THIS BIRTHDAY BOOK

BELONGS TO

_____

POTTER STYLE

Copyright © 2011 by Potter Style,
a division of Random House, Inc.
All rights reserved.
Published in the United States by Potter Style,
an imprint of the Crown Publishing Group,
a division of Random House, Inc., New York.
www.clarksonpotter.com

Printed in China

ISBN: 978-0-307-71981-2

January

It sometimes happens that
a woman is handsomer at twenty-nine
than she was ten years before.

—PERSUASION

January Birthdays

BIRTHSTONE

Garnet

BIRTH FLOWER

Carnation

(A friend in adversity, devoted love, fascination)

ASTROLOGICAL SIGNS

JANUARY 1–20: Capricorn

JANUARY 21–31: Aquarius

JANUARY

1

2

3

4

JANUARY

5

6

7

8

JANUARY

9

10

11

12

Let other pens

dwell on guilt and misery.

—MANSFIELD PARK

JANUARY

13

14

15

16

JANUARY

17

18

19

20

JANUARY

21

22

23

24

JANUARY

25

26

27

28

JANUARY

29 _____

_____

_____

30 _____

_____

_____

31 _____

_____

_____

_____

February

There is
no charm
equal to
tenderness
of heart. . .

— EMMA

February Birthdays

Amethyst

Violet

(Modesty, Faithfulness, Virtue)

FEBRUARY 1–19: Aquarius

FEBRUARY 20–29: Pisces

FEBRUARY

_1_

_2_

_3_

_4_

FEBRUARY

5

6

7

8

FEBRUARY

9

10

11

12

FEBRUARY

13

14

15

16

FEBRUARY

_17_

_18_

_19_

_20_

FEBRUARY

21

22

23

24

25 _____

_____

_____

26 _____

_____

_____

27 _____

_____

_____

28/29 _____

_____

_____

March

An artist cannot do anything slovenly.

—MANSFIELD PARK

March Birthdays

BIRTHSTONE

Aquamarine

BIRTH FLOWER

Daffodil

(Sympathy, Regard, Affection)

ASTROLOGICAL SIGNS

MARCH 1–21: Pisces

MARCH 22–31: Aries

MARCH

1

2

3

4

MARCH

5

6

7

8

MARCH

_9_

_10_

_11_

_12_

MARCH

13

14

15

16

MARCH

17

18

19

20

One half of the world

cannot understand

the pleasures of the other . . .

—EMMA

MARCH

_21_

_22_

_23_

_24_

MARCH

25

26

27

28

MARCH

_29_

_30_

_31_

NOTES

April

A person who can write a long letter
with ease, cannot write ill.

—PRIDE AND PREJUDICE

April Birthdays

BIRTHSTONE

Diamond

BIRTH FLOWER

Daisy
(Bliss, Innocence, Purity)

ASTROLOGICAL SIGNS

APRIL 1–20: Aries

APRIL 21–30: Taurus

APRIL

1

2

3

4

APRIL

5

6

7

8

APRIL

9

10

11

12

APRIL

13

14

15

16

APRIL

17

18

19

20

If you observe, people always

live for ever when there is an

annuity to be paid them.

—SENSE AND SENSIBILITY

APRIL

_21_

_22_

_23_

_24_

APRIL

25

26

27

28

APRIL

29 _____

_____

_____

_____

30 _____

_____

_____

_____

NOTES

May

To sit in the shade on a fine day, and look upon verdure is the most perfect refreshment.

—MANSFIELD PARK

May Birthdays

Emerald

Lily of the Valley
(Hope, Sweetness, Humility)

MAY 1–21: Taurus

MAY 22–31: Gemini

MAY

_1_

_2_

_3_

_4_

MAY

5

6

7

8

MAY

9

10

11

12

MAY

13

14

15

16

MAY

_17_

_18_

_19_

_20_

Friendship is certainly

the finest balm

for disappointed Love.

—NORTHANGER ABBEY

MAY

21

22

23

24

MAY

25

26

27

28

MAY

29

30

31

NOTES

June

There is nothing like
staying home for real comfort.

— EMMA

June Birthdays

Pearl

Rose
(Love, Devotion, Affection)

JUNE 1–22: Gemini

JUNE 23–30: Cancer

JUNE

1

2

3

4

JUNE

5

6

7

8

JUNE

9

10

11

12

JUNE

13

14

15

16

JUNE

17

18

19

20

JUNE

21

22

23

24

JUNE

25

26

27

28

JUNE

29

30

NOTES

July

Nobody minds having
what is too good for them.

—PERSUASION

July Birthdays

Ruby

Larkspur
(Laughter, Happiness, Purity of Heart)

JULY 1–22: Cancer

JULY 23–31: Leo

JULY

1 _____

2 _____

3 _____

4 _____

JULY

5

6

7

8

JULY

9

10

11

12

JULY

13

14

15

16

JULY

17

18

19

20

A lady's imagination

is very rapid; it jumps

from admiration to love,

from love to matrimony

in a moment.

—SENSE AND SENSIBILITY

JULY

21

22

23

24

JULY

25

26

27

28

JULY

29 _____

_____

_____

30 _____

_____

_____

31 _____

_____

_____

_____

August

Silly things do
cease to be silly
if they are done
by sensible
people in an
impudent way.

— EMMA

August Birthdays

Peridot

Poppy

(Grace, Strength of Character, Imagination)

AUGUST 1–23: Leo

AUGUST 24–31: Virgo

AUGUST

1

2

3

4

AUGUST

5

6

7

8

AUGUST

_9_

_10_

_11_

_12_

AUGUST

13

14

15

16

AUGUST

17

18

19

20

We have all a

better guide in ourselves,

if we would attend to it,

than any other person can.

— MANSFIELD PARK

AUGUST

_21_

_22_

_23_

_24_

AUGUST

25

26

27

28

AUGUST

29

30

31

NOTES

September

I declare after all
there is no enjoyment
like reading!
How much sooner
one tires of anything
than of a book!

—PRIDE AND PREJUDICE

September Birthdays

BIRTHSTONE

Sapphire

BIRTH FLOWER

Aster
(Daintiness, Dedication, Affection)

ASTROLOGICAL SIGNS

SEPTEMBER 1–23: Virgo

SEPTEMBER 23–30: Libra

SEPTEMBER

1

2

3

4

SEPTEMBER

5

6

7

8

SEPTEMBER

9

10

11

12

SEPTEMBER

13

14

15

16

SEPTEMBER

17

18

19

20

SEPTEMBER

21

22

23

24

SEPTEMBER

25

26

27

28

SEPTEMBER

29 _____

_____

_____

30 _____

_____

_____

_____

NOTES

_____

_____

_____

_____

October

Everybody likes to go their own way—to choose their own time and manner of devotion.

—MANSFIELD PARK

October Birthdays

BIRTHSTONE

Opal

BIRTH FLOWER

Cosmos
(Joy, Modesty, Appreciation)

ASTROLOGICAL SIGNS

OCTOBER 1–23: Libra

OCTOBER 24–31: Scorpio

OCTOBER

1

2

3

4

OCTOBER

5

6

7

8

OCTOBER

9

10

11

12

OCTOBER

13

14

15

16

OCTOBER

17

18

19

20

It is a truth

universally acknowledged,

that a single man

in possession of a good fortune,

must be in want of a wife.

—PRIDE AND PREJUDICE

OCTOBER

_21_

_22_

_23_

_24_

OCTOBER

25

26

27

28

OCTOBER

29

30

31

NOTES

November

I do not want people to be very agreeable, as it saves me the trouble of liking them a great deal.

—*personal correspondence*

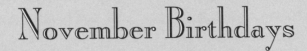

November Birthdays

BIRTHSTONE

Topaz

BIRTH FLOWER

Chrysanthemum
(Cheerfulness, Loveliness, Wealth)

ASTROLOGICAL SIGNS

NOVEMBER 1–22: Scorpio

NOVEMBER 23–30: Sagittarius

NOVEMBER

1

2

3

4

5

6

7

8

NOVEMBER

_9_

_10_

_11_

_12_

NOVEMBER

13

14

15

16

NOVEMBER

17

18

19

20

21

22

23

24

NOVEMBER

25

26

27

28

NOVEMBER

29 _____
_____
_____

30 _____
_____
_____
_____

NOTES

_____
_____
_____
_____

December

How quick
come the
reasons for
approving
what we like!

—PERSUASION

December Birthdays

BIRTHSTONE

Turquoise

BIRTH FLOWER

Narcissus

(Egotism, Foresight, Good Wishes)

ASTROLOGICAL SIGNS

DECEMBER 1–22: Sagittarius

DECEMBER 22–31: Capricorn

DECEMBER

1

2

3

4

DECEMBER

5

6

7

8

DECEMBER

9

10

11

12

DECEMBER

13

14

15

16

DECEMBER

_17_

_18_

_19_

_20_

For what do we live

but to make sport

for our neighbors

and laugh at them

in our turn?

—PRIDE AND PREJUDICE

DECEMBER

21

22

23

24

DECEMBER

25

_____

_____

_____

26

_____

_____

_____

27

_____

_____

_____

28

_____

_____

_____

DECEMBER

29 _____

_____

_____

30 _____

_____

_____

31 _____

_____

_____

_____

GIFT NOTES

Why not seize the pleasure at once?—
How often is happiness destroyed by preparation,
foolish preparations.

—EMMA